Never As Strangers

This book is dedicated to several people who dropped bombs on me and made me change my life:

Dr. Ben
John Henrik Clarke
Frances Cress Welsing
Sonia Sanchez
Haki Madhubuti
Malcolm X & the
Honorable Marcus Garvey

The following poems are dedicated to:

ASCAC / Isisara, Roderick & Art • **Babas** / Rex and Terry • **Libation** / Diop • **A Record Of Ancestral Moans & Groans** / The Last Poets • **That Girl** / My Father • **Ornithology** / Charlie Parker • **Eclipse In Aswan** / James • **Who Was That Masked Man** / Sean • **Never As Strangers** / C.M. • **Curse Of The Bald Head** / Ken • **Too Much Drama For Me** / Ken • **Just How Traditional Do We Spoze To Be** / Amani • **No More Cannabalism** / Rose • **Jam** / Chico Freeman & Billy Harper • **White Traditions In Black-Face** / John Henrik Clarke

NEVER AS STRANGERS

Laini Mataka

W.M. DuForcelf / Baltimore

Published by W. M. DuForcelf

Library of Congress Catalog Card Num. 88-82280
ISBN: 0-933-12175X

W. M. DuForcelf is an imprint of
Black Classic Press

Founded in 1978, the Press specializes in bringing to light obscure and
significant works by and about people of African descent. If our books
are not available in your area, ask your local bookseller to order them.
Our current list of titles can be obtained by writing:

Black Classic Press
c/o List
P.O. Box 13414
Baltimore, MD 21203

TABLE OF CONTENTS

Laini Mataka: In the Tradition

The river of modern Black women poets is thick with quality, enthusiasm, insight and energy. The poetry of Angela Jackson, Ruth Garnett, Sandra Jackson-Opoku and Estella Conwill Alexander all follow and complement the steps of Gwendolyn Brooks, Margaret Walker , Mari Evans, Sonia Sanchez, Lucille Clifton, Jayne Cortez and others. This is not to imply that young Black women poets have not been influenced and nurtured by Black male poets; but it is to suggest that the voices of Black women writers have finally fought their way into the Black and American literary canon, and will never be back-seated again. Laini Mataka, in her book, Never As Strangers, continues the flow of literary disruptions for which Black writers are known .

Of the experienced writers mentioned, she is fine-tuned in the tradition of Sonia Sanchez and Jayne Cortez. The rich rawness that she displays also reminds one of Amiri Baraka and Larry Neal. She has a drum inside her and her words dance with unusual wisdom:

> don't be afraid to tell yr children who the enemy is cuz if you
> don't... the enemy will tell'em its u
> or
> children do not sin
> they imitate

She is a feeling , caring poet and her emotions— often riveting and deep— ride with each poem. She is also very cultural, i.e., intelligent, which makes her an effective political word-carrier. She is a strong, from-the-gut writer. It is evident that she has been "around the block" too many times, and therefore, is able to look destruction in the eye and find bright tomorrows even as she fears the coming day. Her work engages the reader and in each poem of this important book, especially the longer works, she will leave an imprint on the consciousness of her readers.

Ms. Mataka is more of a prose-poet than a close-to-the-chest word-user. Her longer pieces are, in fact, poetic prose and can be loosely classified as poetic essays. She displays the wit and political conscious-ness of a June Jordan and the warmth and hugging care of Lucille Clifton. She writes about Black men with a critical, yet loving and cunning eye. It is enough to just say that she is accurate, especially in the poem, 'Nobody Even Bothered:"

nobody ever told him
nowhere along the booby-trapped road of his life,
did anyone ever tell him that there was some otha way to live
and, that that otha way, was open to him.
nobody ever tried to make him believe that inferiority was not his
destiny.

In "Who Was That Masked Man?," she is able to cut into the surface of male-female relationships while understanding the dangers that such relationships can generate. If she sumbits, more often than not, some-thing greater is lost:

he is her sweetnighter
the night is self-indulgent
as he unfolds himself into the pit of her highest burning
Blackness churnin. he willingly enters in search of
that which his soul craves the most
but his mind will never understand.

Her use of punctuation reminds one of the way musicians use spaces, pauses and off rhythms. Just as you think she is going in one direction, she reverses or goes sideways. Her experimentation with African American English may be appreciated by older readers but will give inexperienced readers some difficulty. However, this language does help to legitimize her message. This is very clear in "A Trip All Sistahs Must Take" and "Somebody's Always Bad Mouthin Blackmen." These two poems give us the thoughts of a woman who has been tested and who is now writing the exam:

He as on loveboat, as on fantasy island
as in ebony's most eligible...is not coming.
but the future still is, so one by one
we've all gotta decide which way to flow since the great HE
probably aint gonna show. shld we pretend we dont kno and spend
the next ten, twenty years makin luv to men who pretend to be
lovers
of something otha than themselves? will our temperatures rise so
high that we take to the sky like vultures ready to land on anything
male?
will our minds go delirious with fever, forcing us out into the
streets to play meat for stray dogs seeking tender flesh to satisfy
their low-life media-induced desires?
AND,
give thanx to bros who tell the police nothing. yesterday, today and
tomorrow too, divine thanx
to those who will die and have died rather than betray Black
secrets.
give thanx for the bros who are self-employed and the inspiration
they give us all as we struggle to be self-reliant.
and give thanx everlasting to
any and all bros who have paid
the extravagant cost of being bros
no matter how high the bill.

This type of finality and insight comes through in much of her poetry.

The real beauty in Never As Strangers is its clearness. She is writing for readers as well as non-readers. This book will have some difficulty winning literary prizes, but in the contest for readers, it will do well.

Much of this work should be set to music. As I read these poems, the power of the collective message reminded me of the work of Gil Scott-Heron.

Laini Mataka's work is in keeping with the best of Black Nationalist writing. However, this work cannot be, and should not be, rejected (or, in the literary community— patronized) because of its political and cultural positions. She is a mature poet who is long overdue for recognition, praise and support. She is a maintainer with vision. I see in her work from "White Traditions in Black-Face," to the title poem "Never As Strangers," a complete repertory of one woman's travels through Black America. It is quite a trip; she says it best:

> *we must*
> *never*
> *half-heartedly smile the dead smile*
> *of patronizing lovers,*
> *never.*

Haki R. Madhubuti

almost ONE THOUSAND *strong,*
    we hit Egypt
like a black tornado.

almost ONE THOUSAND *strong, we*
welcomed our ownselves
back into the wombs we'd all been searching for.

almost ONE THOUSAND *strong, we ran on short fuses,*
w/out physically abusing one anotha.

    and we wordlessly knew
    that we were enacting history— directing the river
    of time
    to turn around our own bend.

almost ONE THOUSAND *strong,*

we ran into our ancestors' open arms
though some thought we were just sight-seeing
we allowed ourselves to be captives in a glorious
moment of remembering and echoing and resounding.

and then one day when i was sittin in my kitchen
i looked up suddenly and everybody was just...gone.

    no complaining, no laughing, no singing,
no grumbling,
      no rolling of the eyes, no kinship smiles...just gone.

how cld y'all do that to me?

what a pleasure, such sanity
        such graciousness, such maleness.
I am
pleasantly nurtured and cradled in the cornucopia
of yr humbly offered wisdom.
            yr smiles bring me virgin joy
            becuz they evolve in the absence
            of motives.

yr sharing and caring breathes a quality
like gold but far more valuable.

the musik of yr laughter rises mellifluously
timely
and w/out malice.

            there is no calculating the sudden wealth
            yr company has bestowed upon me. i feel
        like a lottery winner of the first degree, 360 degrees
richer.
and in an effort to pay you back
i will be stronger
            and more formidable than
            i've thought myself able to be.

Abu Simbel

my ancestors mourn through stone
their illustriousness profaned and desecrated
by blood-clots whose icy-ness later
cancerized the world.

and yet, the power and brilliance of their AFRIKANESS
defies total obliteration

their voices resist muting.

my fingers, feeling the original braille
traced their granite messages and felt time
whiplash within me
until inflamed memory plucked at the swollen
strings of my heart.

with each step— the recollections grew
every groove, every crack, every indentation,
every crevice told me
        how much i had been missed.

and my tears felt like home-coming drops of blood from
a wound begging to be sealed and healed by a
never-ending-reunion.

and from the holy of holies
came a sacrosanct whisper of welcome
and the solemn placenta-filled promise
that we will never be separated again.
now flesh has meshed into precious stone
        we will never be separated again.

when the sun fell   i moon
streaked across the sky, faster than the speed of light.
    with the intensity of a mother's love
i advanced
        to rescue my source of illumination.

when the sun fell   i moon
gathered clouds in my arms to cushion his head
    and from the depths of my nubian craters
    i urged

        medicinal flows of unending concern
            tributaries of unyielding tenderness.

when the sun fell   i moon
begged the MOST HIGH to lay the descent on me
    that my firebreather might rise and
continue to give life.

    and now that the sun is in his rightful place
    i moon
    must seek my own level by myself, while carrying
    the pyramidal weight of the fact, that
        he doesnt kno me.

Libation

the RAGE of a de-faced ancestor
taught my blood how to boogie messages of death
to anti-life whiteness.
the eternal scream of a de-voiced ancestor
has locked into the valley of my forever hearing
and turned my personal song into something
too crucial even for my own lips to sing.

 but the song
being a mixture of royal menstral blood
and the sperm of shattered kings
is so turbulent a melody that my mouth jammed shut
cant suppress it. and my face drawn rubber-band-tight cant
conceal it. and the voiceless, faceless ancestors
continue to suffer the length of eternity, waiting
for that final Black cleansing action that will release
their souls from the spiritually bankrupt diaspora
and return them to the only home BLACKNESS has
ever known.

crooners w/out form conspire with the nameless many
to make me pay unspeakable dues
(fortunately, i know how to blues)
there is no part of me they wld not use to sound off
about the continuous victimization of the
chosen people— chosen to die in anyway that the
collective white imagination fancies.

the times are increasing when i trip out on history
and come back speakin in tongues not my own
but all mine.
wherever there may be a half an eardrum
the ancestral steering committee beats in my soul
and speaks thru me, turning any and every conversation
into a lecture, a prayer for all the scattered
Black children
to scatter back to Blackness for humanity's sake
       for Afrika's sake
       for our children's sake
come
let us flick the eternal switch that lights up the world.
who amongst u wld come
add yr hearts beating to the wardrums
be the war
or be the drum?
just come...

A Record Of
Ancestral Moans & Groans

the griot shld be killed that doesnt state
authoritatively, that Black people never sang the blues
til they met white people.

  and from there we sang the blues all the way across the
atlantic. we sang the blues from the FREEDOMZONES
of the tiger sharks bellies. from every auction block we
moaned the blues to mourn the loss of the DRUM.
while the names of our gods were branded and
traumatized out of our collective minds, we sang the blues to
think that the ancestors cldnt find us.
we sang the blues with every forced migration.
we sang the blues thru proxy emancipation. we sang the
blues to RECONSTRUCT ourselves and then we echo'd
the blues using our blood to seal a stolen nation.

  we sang the blues while choking on the GLITTERING
PUS of the promised land. yes, we sang the blues
in every urban dream that was ever mistaken for a life;
& we sang the blues of integration, & our tears put the
civil rights acts to musik (a musikal comedy).
we sang the blues til it became our nat'l
anthem and cried the blues behind every election as we
marched flat-footed into every war while being lynched
on every otha tree. and we sang the blues from
overseas where we pumped death into the enemy
as pointed out to us by our enemies.
and we sang the dupe'd blues when we came home to
find we had NO HOME just as before.

with my man in my throat, i sang the blues where
anybody cld hear me, and carry my messages to him;
wherever he was. i sang the blues becuz i wanted to be
a woman, and then i sang the blues for real becuz
i already was.

i sang the blues while climbing into the stirrups for a
whether report and i sang the blues thru all the early
morning departures... embryonic and full grown.
i sang the blues behind the weight of a pregnant shadow
sliding across my wall as i paced u in & out of my life
past, present and future.

i sang the blues in whitey's kitchens while
campaigning against the rats in my own. i sang the blues
behind premature births a hundred years, too early six
hundred years, too late. i sang the blues in courtroom
dramas that threaten'd to take my only child who was my
only sanity and i sang the blues older than water as i
buried my sistah next to my son, and across from my
daughter. i sang the blues where only white folks cld
hear me, in tones that only their deaths cld comprehend.
i sang the blues and i washed the blues and i ate, slept
and excreted the blues becuz my GODS refused
to answer and my man wld not come home.

i sang the blues thru more winters than amerika can
even dream up and i used those same blues to keep
myself warm thru all those blue-black empty nites.
and i sang the blues, cuz that was the ony way i cld
neutralize what i knew they were trying to do to my soul.

8

and i sang the blues where ever there was a taste to tell
time by. i sang the blues behind institutional doors
all night longgggg. i have cried the blues, lived, luv'd
and died the blues, and now?

now, i say later for being blue.
cuz i dont want nothin in my life that aint positively
    BLACK.

George

this poem does not commemorate ghosts
ghosts being a white mans conception of a
universal entity.
this poem will key the unlocked spirit of
george jackson
           (jonathan being a whole otha testament)
this poem
is a demonstration; designed to re-expose the
primitiveness of white people who still dont kno that it's
time to come outa that cro-magnon shit.

        they laid for him.
forced him to play the victim for the last time
and even after they filled his body with lead
and was sure he had to be dead. dead. dead.
they handcuffed him.
afraid even of his spirit
that it might fly up outa his body
and avenge it.
they tried to capture his soul in death,
since they were never able to do it in life.
and they left his body bakin
away in the sun for six hours
to be sure he was no longer a threat.
but little did they kno
that his people had feasted on his dreams
and drank deep the blood in his eye,
to later go out into the nite
lookin for somethin white
        to mutually sacrifice.

D'Joint

I

courtside:
becuz there is no reason to rise
new days are raped of their potential
and left dying like crust
on some waking, tho non-seeing eye.

II

steel and concrete do not inspire growth
in any living thing
within their confines
flowers die
and men wither.

III

on the otha side of prison walls
my heart splinters into a thousand sunless cells.

IV

the man of my dreams wears a montage
of convict faces. and these hours spent in
yearning, form bars
as hard as the ones that imprison my lover's face.

like a premature grave-robber
she stole big momma thornton's voice;
siphoned out the anguish, dried it up, snorted it,
and went out into the raw lookin
for something Black to squeeze.

she wanted to experience the niggerness of life
w/out the peculiar consequences, of course.
she wanted to plug into that electricity that seemed to
run so unchecked among those magnificent darkies.
she wanted to make soundz like the enslaved, the raped,
the castrated, the mutilated, the hunted, the lynched.
she wanted her voice to sound like it came from the
cotton or tobacco fields, or from the shacks of mighty
men being kicked outa their beds by massah.
it seems she had this little known dream to star as
the mulatto in a reverse version of IMITATION OF LIFE.
and, the best way for her to pick up on some quick soul
was some Black jank...
so when bigger thomas caught her eye, she knew
she had found her man. and in the still of a hot-laced nite
he janked her up. sd. here it is, bitch. take it.
this is what u want, aint it, aint it?
and madam gagged and gasped for breath while bein
shot up with 2,000 seasons of pure Blackness! 400 years
of devastation! and the pain was so good, she came. and
died. in a sleasy situation, amidst cheap thrills and
gutbucket dreams of seeing the real big momma
thornton face-to-face and gettin a good ass-whippin!

the de-mystification of demons
goes as such:
> *first.*

the
wite boy
is
not
a
god ... like anyone else
him
can
be
wasted.

It's All Right To Let Some People Into Yr Vestibule, But Never In Yr Livingroom

PEOPLE, sometimes they come into yr life w/out a clear
      understanding of their own.
PEOPLE, sometimes they come into yr life w/out half an
      idea about what effect they wld like to cause.
PEOPLE, sometimes they be harboring a benign-kind
      of chaos which they inject into yr life as well.
PEOPLE, sometimes be so diligent in their pursuit of
      what they think they want from u, that they totally
over-look the damage that their selfishness can inflict on
your feelings.
where there are no ground rules, confusion has a warm
place to grow.
where there are no ground rules, misinterpretation has
its own olympics.
where there are no ground rules, harmony is a drunken
driver.

and sometimes, people open their hearts to a lover just
to find
      they've let in a stranger
and sometimes, people tell their minds to shut-up and let
their
      hearts take the floor
and sometimes, people can see the twisted arrow of fate
comin right
      at'em but their karma makes them
freeze and take the hit!

14

and sometimes, people forget themselves, just to please
othas
tho othas never forget themselves to please
and sometimes, people be so enraptured in what they
feel to be luv
      that they fail to consider who is doing the luvin.

where there are no ground rules, assumptions overwork
the mind
where there are no ground rules, pain is a game-hunter
stalkin for fun
where there are no ground rules, the future is made with
match sticks
      that any sudden truth can blow away.

To Black Rapists and Anyone Else
Who Just Wants To Have A Good Time

hard as i be luvin u, i still gotta fear u most of the
time. i gotta fear u lookin at me too hard. gotta
fear u askin me my name. gotta fear u wantin to kno
where i live. i gotta fear u findin me and lyin to
me and trying to drape me and tryin to take over my
space. tryin to get over and on top of me. i be luvin
u close up and faraway at the same time. from times
present and eons past i be luvin the sheer electricity
of u doing right and givin the world its balance with yr
pyramidal-revolutionary miracles. yet, hard as i be
luving u, if u ever pick me to act out yr hatred upon,
i will NOT be sympathetic. i will not brotherize u.
i will not be fair. i will not be victim.
if u mean to hurt me, then i mean to kill u
and i will be just as serious as u are!

How Come U Aint Got No Children
And What Chu Waiting For?

Never enuff. how cld there ever be enuff luv
to insure that my life whip harmony outa all this chaos?
    everything that i am
    I have been too often.

the luv of one man cld never be enuff.
i have been capitalistically robbed of the luv,
togetherness, and devotion of thousands of Blackmen.
and the luv of one man cld never really be enuff
to make me feel secure enuff to have a baby.

        i need a whole community of bros
        to promise me they'll cherish me

and be bro to me
as i have been all things of luv to them.
then, and only then wld i
roll the sacred stone away from the entrance to my
royal birth chamber, and make ready to suckle a world
        that cannot be compromised.

SOS: Wld Somebody Please Help Sheena Keep Her Clothes On

there is something very un-complimentary bout the way
some Black women allow themselves to be seen as in all
ovah, as in too little, trying unsuccessfully to cover too
much.

is it any wonder, when they walk the streets, they are
mistaken for street-walkers. foreign eyes run
up and down those Blk thighs like the eyes of customers
checkin out a piece of rumproast.

some sistahs wear their skin for show. believin thats
what most bros want, they circle their eyes with blue
majik, smudge their cheeks with rouge, smear their lips
with purple raindrops, and begin to audition for a chance
to mean something to somebody. the brutal dawn of too
many mornings exposes them as transparent kicks
which when totaled are never worth the time or the lines
deepening in their faces.

some sistahs specialize in houdini antics by managing to
get into jeans two sizes too small w/out grease.
the hipsters jackets, naturally made for hipsters, will
always put the emphasis on the butt. and some sistahs
be walkin round with their cheeks lookin like melons
trying to bust outa the jordache horse's eye. and even the
most righteous bro is bound to feel a slight twinge
simply becuz nature responds to nature.

now even tho i seem to be talkin bout sistahs, the real
issue here is where are the real Black men? those capable
of perceiving and intervening in this mess. where are the
real Black men, when these sistahs be reveling in their
essence magazine-mania. where are the real Black men,
strong enuff to suppress their own carnal appetites long
enuff, to help some sistahs correct their showcase
images of self before they end up back on the auction
block? the intervention of these bros. is crucial to
Black womanhood; and therefore vital to the Black
everthing-hood. real Black men are needed to assist in
the strengthening of real Black women, who, if
left alone in their current state of confusion
will be doomed to cruise their lives away
on ships that never anchor.

everyday she stroked him, pumped his head wide open
with surrealistic feelings of gusto,
made him think he was younger than his body cld afford
to be.
and everyday he just laid back, lettin her have her
slimy way with him. burning out his brain with the
frosty strokes of her pale fingers.
eroding his nasal passages til future voyages became
impossible.
and still, he wanted her no matter what it cost
to keep her
his every vein cried to her for fulfillment.
every opening was jammed shut awaiting
         her cooling touch
and for every one step they took together, death
took two.
the final hours were ugliness magnified into HBO:
the stealing, the conniving, the sucking of otha people's
blood, the disintegration of the appearance,
the permanent ashiness of the skin, the babbling, the
jerkiness, the paranoia, the scurrying around rat-like
chasing her down without shame, without any memory
of right or wrong, or family and friends.

he only socialized intraveneously.
and the last time he saw her she was wearing a new
shade of brutality, ripped his arteries open,
bludgeoned his heart, beat
his immune system to the ground.

and still, he clinged to her legs
   when she tried to kick him away.

nobody ever told him.
no where along the booby-trapped road of his life,
did anyone ever tell him that there was some otha way to
live and, that that otha way, was open to him.
nobody ever tried to make him believe that inferiority
was not his destiny.

nobody ever told him what he was good for, or at. and all
he ever knew was what he cldnt do. nobody ever showed
him how to use the flow of time. not go against it. a little
work, or even a lot, probably cld have changed all the
things he was bad at, to things he cld do, if he wanted to.

nobody ever told him that success wears a mask, and
that is not her true face. reggie jackson was not born
playing baseball in his motha's womb. he had to learn.
and then he had to work at what he learned...and the rest
is his-story. but nobody ever told him that work was not
somethin to fear hate and reject. nobody ever even tried
to make him see that anybody he admired and wanted to
be like had to work hard to be good at whatever it was
they did that he thought was so hip.

and nobody ever told him that life cld be collared and
brought down to eye level. that success wasnt nothin but
a dance. and anybody who cld handle breakin,
poppin and lockin, cld also handle algebra, chemistry,
and computers.

nobody ever pulled him up, not one time...was he told
that dreams are made to possibly come true. they may
not always be able to feed u, but u cant live w/out them.
and u dont have to.

if i had known him i wld have told him to find something
to luv, and master it. learn to luv to use yr mind like u love
to work that body. but, i didnt kno him.

but it was obvious that nobody had ever told him, that he
was worth more than any thing he cld ever want. and he
never gave himself credit for anything.

so death was not unexpected. it came violently.
he went out obscenely.
w/out ever being told.

Only Blood Can Fill
The Brand New Beggar's Cup

spirits enjoy the cloak of darkness, thats why they go
visiting at nite.
if they come knockin in the middle of one of yr nites, and
u decide to let them in
they'll be knockin on yr door, forever.
u will never again be able to ignore them and live
comfortably with yrself at the same time.
for as u lean yr head away from their timeless knocking, u
will also be leaning farther away from yr pt of origin.
time will prove unworthy of yr trust. bazaarness will be
peeking in and outa the windows of yr soul if u do not let
the spirits enter and have their ancestral way with u.
they will increase in number.
and yr nites will be constantly broken up by their cries for
justice.
yr days will grow longer as they ride u into the ground
demanding reparations. and as long as u try
to out-distance them there will be no peace the distance
of anywhere u might run.

so if spirits come knockin in the nite, dont bother to
panic...dont reach for a light...just let'em flow on in.
what they want from u is probably more purposeful than
what u want from yrself. and if u havent started already,
its time to ante-up   OR
like the temptations shlda said,
   "if its blood that u're running from
            there's no hidin place."

it is so hard to be earth bound
when yr wings are aching to challenge the high-tide
of a revolutionary wind.
so hard to remain terrestrial when the skin remembers
being bird. and the heart soars back and forth in its
ribbed cage...
the song of the crow gives rebirth to a lonliness that
manifests itself in the flight-time of the life-time.
it is so hard to be earthbound
wings dragging beside u on the ground
u cld lift them if folks wld just get off of 'em.
they kno u're dependable so they lean on u
hopin to be included on yr next flight.
and not being able to take off gives u the woes
occasionally u claw at what loves u the most
and everything u sing after that is beyond even the blues.

so much is lost when the lost claim to be the only thing
happenin. they eat, sleep, and excrete in fear of being genetically
assassinated. the unsurpassed splendor of our united plummage makes
them plot to slaughter the bird in us. their media tells us to hate the sky.
they make us think that stagnation is better than flight of any kind,
motion of any sort. they trick us into turning in our wings. and they burn

the wings that are not turned in.

but sometimes, the way we can feel about each otha is totally
regenerating to the most scorched wings.

the right look, an opening smile that never closes,
sometimes, the way we dare to feel about each otha, is
all the flight-times of the most magnificent birds in all
the worlds where luv and freedom are a way of being.
sometimes, we do that to each otha.

wanna fly?

M&M'S

just imagine what cldve happened if mike & michael
were even a little bit afro-centric. they cldve put
their nappty heads together and decided between the
two of them who wld win. then they cldve gotten
a tip to the Black community about who to bet on.
together they cldve bet on the chosen winner, and
cleaned up.
later, they cldve scheduled a rematch and done the
same thing, without tellin white folks ANYTHING.

w/out a space to call yr own
    u are homeless. weighing nothing
    meaning less.
w/out a space to occupy
  u float in and out of yrself
  unattached— fragmented
    a solo creature w/out
      the power to
      harness yr own energy and make
a safe get-a-way.

that the ones with vaginas must concede

is an ancient mandate

> that has been handed down
> since the beginning of time

written on scrolls of flesh

and tucked away inside the dead penises

of bloodclots who once were men.

Who Was That Masked Man?

he is her sweetnighter
on the right occasion, something fine
to go back and tell home about.
but she has so many backed-up nites to sweeten,
can the musikman hang?

will his understanding of sound do any good
in turning her head around when the
midnight special be passin thru,
hurrying on to play the main attraction
in someone else's blues?

can he rock her steady enuff to pull from her the
deepest tones (the proper moans)?
            the night is self-indulgent
        as he unfolds himself into the pit of her highest
burnings, Blackness churnin.
he willingly enters in search of
            that which his soul craves the most
                but his mind will never understand.

he fire'd me up
          and told me not
to take it personally,
he fingered the sweetmeat
          (tho it was i who made the feast)
     and with a tongue
that once belonged to the sun
          he flame-licked my temple
     and made it glow
long after all the tongues
and all the suns
          had disappeared.

as if we had never spun sweat
into silk
          on a hot summer nite.
we must
never
half-heartedly smile the dead smile
of patronizing lovers.
never.
          nothing cld be more natural than the
          seizures yr flesh inspired
to be echo'd
again
and again
thru out carnal memory to survive in near-religious
sweetness
to be something
we can never
help smiling about when the memories
come round, beggin for luv.
          so lets cancel out all would be exits...
          once spirits lock-in...divorce is impossible.
so, the two people passing in the street
trying mutually not to see one anotha,
can never be us.
not after what we've been.
the years cld alter my mind but my thighs wld still
remember that once we spun silk on a hot stolen summer
nite. the pattern was mine but it was yr threading
that made it right.

Ido

this song is slow being born becuz
   it comes from inside a part of me
        that i have not investigated yet.
            (i miss u)

who expects to find luv
   exactly as prayed for.
who expects to go way across the world
   to hear a line overly-heard at home
        and still fall for it.
            (i miss u)

twin minutes cant escape w/out u ridin
   somewhere in between lookin as if u really
        mean what you say.
making it hard for me to wander outside of yr eyes,
   and impossible for u to relocate away
        from my main artery.
            (i miss u)

bodies dont lie, and i believed everything u sd.
i never sd enuff.
fortune-telling motives is an art i have not mastered
yet, i believe that
our instincts are the only jewels we really own.
yrs led u right to me
mine let u find me.
        but thousands of miles away
        at home
i wondered about u
yet, when i was filling the space between yr arms
under yr stars
        i never wondered for a moment.

33

And This 30 Days Will Be
No More Eternal Than Any Otha

first of september
he came back
    smiled away yr heart's resistance
he nourished yr soul
and u grew to be
    a lotus blossom out of season.
he came back
to stay u thought
        how cld he ever wanna leave again after
        all the tempestuous sessions of locked
        breath, sweating OUTLOUD, flesh steaming.
    how?
cld he ever wanna hide from yr luv's light
in fearful fright/of having to luv u back.

        it was the perfect days that brought him back
        the lying sigh of september promising to stay
        and never even sojourning long enuff
for unconscious luv to regain its senses.

it was the flawlessly beautiful skies, the fierce burning
of the sun on the run to radiate someone else's fragile world.

it was the leaves turning that made him come back
the invigorating air, the illusion of youthful strength
regained.
        it was the clean-smell of cool good-sleeping
        nites and the drunken remembrance of big-legged
        sapphires and the truth behind the legends.

it was
september that he really came back for
u just happened to be there when he got there
                              (again).

All Black Men
Are My Husbands

     his penis
        is really a snake and
we
are really in haiti
        and i
am really
a priestess
        and DAMBALLAH
           is really my father;
        i kiss his namesake,
        and what i urge to flow
has been called
        rivers.

I

even in sleep   u wrap yrself around me
real anaconda-like   afraid to lose me
even in dreams. yet, deep down inside
some part of me cant wait for u to
go to sleep   so it can get away.

II

my spirit wanted u
and made it look as if flesh
was the one that called.

III

luvin u is not necessarily needin u, is not
being possessed by u   is merely a joyful
acknowledgement of yr existence.

luving u is not necessarily wantin u but
more like wantin to celebrate u w/out
u even having to be here to mess things up.
*   in otha words,*
my luv
already has a strong backbone and
doesnt need yr support   to survive.

*   what i feel for u is real   i cant deny it*
*   and u cant exploit it.*

so she sd, if u lose me, u lose a good thing.
and he sd, u're right
but there are so many good things
what cld the loss of one good thing be to me.
and she sd yeah, somebody else may groove u, but
nobody will ever luv u like i do.
and he sd, baby that might be true
but the things that these young girls can do, make
a man like me forget about luv   and u.
and she sd, well if u feel like that   f--k u too
and before she cld make it to the door   he was at
his usual place on the floor cryin:

    baby, c'mon baby
and baby wld come
all week, until he messed things up
by stayin out all night.
mornin wld break un-evenly
and she wld say,

    u kno, if u lose me....

u want me now
that the world has turned out not
to be yr oyster.
u want to possess even my imperfections
if they'll keep u from feeling alone.
but alone
is where u need to be with a broken t. v.
and nothing   but the sound of god's voice
*   in yr steel-plated head.*
u have not lived with a sensitive enuff awareness
of otha people's feelings and yr curse is
to luv a dread woman who DREADS u not.

Fooled U

sometimes,
        discovering luv is not so much a beautiful thing.
sometimes,
        it makes yr heart say "oh shit"
cuz this time
luv
        was not where u wanted to go.

u wanted to work up a sweat
take a shower
and wing out on an empty promise.

u wanted to bask in its glow, get a quick tan
and then head on out for somebody else's space

        anywhere, but luv.

u wanted to be adored and turned loose;
SATED and eternally appreciated,
but somehow the equation failed.

and with yr usual flair and flawless sense of timing
u disengaged yr body and freed it for its next episode
        but yr heart, stayed!
    plunging u into the real-life horror of having to
need, someone else...
        and luv was not where u wanted to go
        this time, but helllllo.

sometimes
> luv does not last forever.

and its nobody's fault.
better to cherish, even what u imagine to be luv...
its wiser to bottle all that u can squeeze from that dream
> come true, and put it some place close
>> to where u burn the most.

and when luv seems not to last as long as the one
who
luv'd the most, had planned,
what good does it do to strip images from the flesh of
memory?
what difference does it make, why, it happened?
isnt the happening in itself, enuff
> to make u wanna beat blood outa glass
>> with raw fists and then fall
>>> to yr knees, thanking GOD
for allowing the ache of such a one-time-only
encounter?

Too Much Drama For Me

bloodclot.
    thinx hes stanley kawolski
    thinx my locks belong to stella
    thinx its normal to be trapped on a
streetcar named desire.
    thinx arguing is sensuous
    finds threats stimulatin
    likes to keep shit goin, then
jump in the sack
fuck incredibly
then wallow in the juice of his own pleasure.

well, my name aint stella
im not pregnant
and my sis's name aint blanche

so if its a fight he wants,
trying to oppress me will get it.
and if he wants to make threats,
only a fool wld warn the person hes about to harm.

u cant dump on me and then jump on me.
mental cruelty doesnt make me wet
for the body that wld just as soon bash me
as caress me.

and dont no streetcars run round my way, anyway.

Just How Traditional
Do We Spoze To Be

sometimes, relatin to some bros (esp. from otha
countries) is like dealin with neanderthals: a club on the
head, the drag of an ass, and true love abounds.

the only time they want u to be a woman is in bed
otherwise, be obedient, be humble, be quiet, be stupid,
disappear (but don't take the puss).

that u cld entertain a thought and attract a sperm at the
same time, is inconceivable. everybody knos that
menstruation destroys brain cells over a long period of
time.

be a woman who earns her own money, be a woman
who's aware of her own sexuality, be a woman who can
hold her own in most conversations, and u will be a
woman ALONE.

what we (Black she and he)
have been to each otha is the luv story of the world's
evolution.
he who controlled the purse strings did not control all
things.
a sense of balance was our gift from the Gods
and we gave it up at the evil insistence of some
red-neck
        muthafuckas who just happen'ed to be passin
        thru AFRIKA.

and now u wanna ignore even the most blatant of
facts.
here in 1987   u still wanna talk about a woman's place:
   After one of the Candace queens personally
challenged alexander the great at ethiopia's border
   After Nzinga used all aspects of her female self to
fight and keep the portuguese out of angola
   After Yaa encouraged the sisters to kick ass and take
their Ghanaian-ness back
   After Harriet tripped and tricked white death outa
several hundred slaves, whom she personally freed
in spite of her sleeping fits
   After my grandmotha worked 12 and 13 hrs daily in
otha peoples' kitchens and singly raised the last of six
kids and then me
   YOU wanna tell me about a woman's place. After i
been takin care of myself for over 12 years, being totally
and
completely responsible for my own self— honey,
the next time u say something to me about a woman's
place
u'd better be asking a question!

every inch of space i occupy is a woman's place.
everywhere i dare to stride is a woman's place.
everywhere i lay my head, every where i wrap my legs,
everywhere i spread my dreads, is a woman's place.

anywhere i shake my butt, anywhere i leave a thought,
anywhere i leave a drop of blood, anywhere i conceive or
delete is a woman's place.

44

anywhere i leave a footprint, a fingerprint, a body print,
an image, or a scent is a woman's place...and i'm talkin
history here.
except for where penises bloom, sho me a space that's
not a woman's place and i'll show u where u lost yr mind.

u cant devour me anymore.
    cant take pieces of me into yrself to gain strength.
    to run off and ambush some otha sistah.
no more cutting up and cutting out
    my vital organs to make musik out of
    and sell to strangers w/out offering me a dimes
    worth of "hello"
no more gorgin on what u like while
    the better parts dry up and cry away.
    anybody wants some of me gonna havta take
        the whole pie.
      cuz aint no lotsa pieces of me gonna be floating
round.
so,
    those of u thats already gotta slice of my life
    savor it honey, and give thanx
    cuz the only thing im givin up these days is
WHOLENESS
      AND THE RAPTURE THEREIN.

Reflections

we shld be havin the time of our lives
rockin
til the early morning hours, laughin home
with the masculines of our choice. steada
watching the late movie
reading the best seller (among singles)
and rememberin the runnings
                before AIDS.

wherever they are now, i'm glad to have touched them all
broad and tall
slender and small, they never burned me.

didnt buy me things
didnt always treat me good, never beat me
didnt always treat me fair, never cursed me
gave me trich twice,
but never gave me a disease that wldnt go away.

and this is a desolate song of gratitude
to the lovers i have known
w/out havin had to pay the ultimate price.

a saxophone player is a woman slayer
relentlessly sought— nightly,
     by women
     with libertine dreams of being unforgettable.

they perfume themselves with exotic delusions,
powder down with unconquerable yearnings.
and carry themselves as if they were
     immaculately conceived.   *and becuz*
   there is
so much sameness, so much grabbing at the same
dream
onli one someone can slip thru the needle's eye
and there is always ONE in the crowd
     whose eyes promise everlastin luv
     and whose inner-doors cant wait to be BLOWN
     off their hinges by some soul-stirring riff

and she firmly believes
that whats going into that horn, that tidal-wave
can somehow, be harnessed and ridden and broken
and made to have eyes onli
     for her.

no ordinary woman
she fantasizes being blown thru her own reed and having herself
played back in tones of yammy-jammy red.

somewhere around the second set
her rising pulse makes her raise her skirt to let the
melody tongue her thighs.
the muscles in her face wrestle
        with the pain and pleasure of wanting
        but not having.
her eyes shine a hundred fires dancing nakedly in
front of a captive lover.
        and the horn can dig it.
cuz the horn helps the BLACKMAN convey to his woman
how it feels not to be able to give her the world.
but

    ooooh, how sweet its gonna be
    when finally, he can.

Somebody's Always
Bad Mouthin Blackmen

and
most of what they say is true
but its not true
about most Blkmen.
     this is a praise-song, hear?
hum a little billy harper to it if u want
but up outa my heart which aint no easy place
i give thanx for the births of all the Black, brown and
   beige bros who struggled to get out of that birth canal
   and have since never tried to re-enter.

give thanx to all the bros who know and have always
   known the value of family as opposed to dropping
   seeds in every reachable field of glory.
give thanx to all the bros who accompany their women
   into the delivery rooms to witness and participate in
   the positive welcoming of their new-born into this
   world.
give thanx to bros who actively join in controlling births
   and preventing diseases.
give thanx to bros who work unbelievable fuckedup jobs
   to secure the needs of their families, esp. the ones who
   thought about runnin but never cld.
give thanx to bros who cook and clean and change
   diapers w/out fear of their dicks fallin off.
give thanx to bros who take care of their children.
give thanx for bros who are actively invovled in the

development of their children— who kno their highs
and lows, their likes and dislikes. special thanx to the
bros who manage this irregardless of their
relationships with the mothas.
give thanx to the bros who save otha bros harvest.
who take the motha and therefore take the
children...whether they are liked by them or not.
these bros dont come in masses but are many enuff to
mention.
give thanx to the bros who have no children but who
treat all of our children like they are all really ours.
and instead of worrying them about the when of
fatherhood, we shld be grateful for the luv they do
share.
give thanx for bros who luv and respect their mothas
and therefore luv and respect Black womanhood.
give thanx to bros who let a woman be herself without
tryin to mold her or shape her into a piss-poor
imitation of a wite girl.
give thanx to bros who like the women they sleep with
and who dont sleep with women they dont like.
give thanx for the bros who have taken the time
and the care to patch up the injuries on the hearts of
sistahs, who ran head-on into the wrong niggah.
give thanx for bros who let Black women be their
friends w/out trying to seduce them farther on
down the road.
give thanx to bros who dont take advantage of women
even when they kno they can...pass up, the
opportunities to pimp no matter how available they
may be.
give thanx to the bros who have never raised their hands

against a woman. let me just back up and give them
some more thanx on that.
give thanx to bros who oppose rape first in their hearts
and who defend Black women w/out having to kno
them. i'm talkin bout those stalkin moments when
sistahs ask unknown bros to walk with them or watch
them to their cars and the average blood who gives her
that coverage w/out a pause.
give thanx to the bros who resisted and do resist
enslavement thru drugs and for the lesser heroes
give thanx also for those who are enslaved, but yet
warn othas about the wicked possibilities. give thanx
for bros who luv otha bros w/out fear of freakiness.
give thanx to bros who tell the police nothing. yesterday,
today and tomorrow too. divine thanx to those who will
die and have died rather thanx than betray Black secrets.
give thanx to bros who receive fame and yet remain
beautifuly true to the race and its image.
give thanx for the bros who are self-employed and the
inspiration they give us all as we struggle to be
self-reliant.
and
give thanx everlasting to any and all bros who have paid
the extravagant cost of being bros
no matter how high the bill.

Afrikansun Rise
&
Give My Regards To Langston

if u really are the sun-rising, please come.
  afrikansunrise, miracle that ive spent the last
    third of my life trying to bring about.
like all the lovers i will never get ovah,
  afrikansunrise, u are breaking my heart
    with this elaborate foreplay.

WHEN
  will u fill my insides with luv: everlastin,
    chakakahn wailing luv? please, if u really
      are what all the garveysdubois's
  lumumbasmalcolmshaki's say u are, please come.
    u are so desperately needed, that some folks
      are gettin scared, and goin back to the
plantations.

  i'm givin out of my every muscle, now.
    cant afford too much for my self, cuz
      u're the one i luv, u're the one i need,
        u're the one my mama always told me wld come
      even tho she thought u'd be a man.

  it has always been u, afrikansunrise. even when
i was back on the plantation, i always knew
    that the kinda life around me wasnt the kinda life
      i intended to live.

didnt none of those rhythms do nothing for my feet.
   so, i left and went lookin for a beat that i cld
      dance to. and didnt nothin in me ever quake, til
         i was visited by u, afrikansunrise.
      and i was born again so many times just knowin u
      were comin, afrikansunrise, just knowin u were
around the eternal bend caused me to dive in
unchartered waters
      for yr namesake.

   and i'm still here, lover.
   waitin and workin. trying to pull up the many curtains,
      so that the world'll be able to dig on yr unveiling.
      aint nobody gonna believe it except those who
      prayed for u to happen; begged for u to come;
      sacrificed everything so u cld have a clear path
      to burst in on, in style, like the sweet tomorrow
morning al jarreau prophesized.
   and a whole lotta people bled oceans of blood to wash
the path u're to come in on and that path, will be the
         mightiest work of luv, the earth has ever seen.
      cuz blood, blood, Blackblood, Black,
Black bloodBlack,
         Blackbloods, died, got shot, got gased
got stabbed, got beat up, got blown up, got locked up,
got lobotomized,
            blood, Black, Black, bloodBlack, Blackblood,
drenched the path, makin it holy for the one and only
afrikansunrise.
      please come. and give us some of everything we will
         ever need; please come.

and if u cant come, tell us thru the ancestors
where u are,
　　　　　and we'll come, and get'chu.

A Trip All Sistahs Must Take

*if we cld turn down the musik for a second. if we cld
turn the videos off for an extended moment. if we cld put down the
beauty magazines forever, and just look each otha square in the face,
then most of us wld have to admit that HE is not coming.
HE as on loveboat, as on fantasy island
as in ebony's most eligible. . . is not coming.
but the future still is, so one by one
we've all gotta decide which way to flow since the great HE probably
aint gonna show. shld we pretend we dont kno and spend the next ten,
twenty years makin luv to men who pretend to be lovers of something
otha than themselves? will our temperatures rise so high that we take to
the sky like vultures ready to land on anything male? will our minds go
delirious with fever forcing us out into the streets to play meat for stray
dogs seeking tender flesh to satisy their low-life media-induced
desires?*

*HE is not coming. but that wont stop time from unfolding and
despite anything we've been told in our lives, a man dont make a
woman. she is herself even when he aint on the scene. and the fact that
she belongs to herself, aint wearing nobody's brandname, does not
make her any less a part of the earth, or any less
spectacular than any of the otha flowers. the fact that no man claims her
does not mean that she is unwanted, or that she shld be pitied. families
are infamous in
reminding their single women of their singleness. some have the nerve to
be embarrassed and are quick to make excuses to explain away her
status.*

*He is not coming. and the panic is on. and some of us
are beginning to look real sly-eyed at each otha's men, wonderin how to*

rationalize our way into a hotshot, which is about the best shot that most
married men can give. and like musikal chairs, we
be playin in and outa one anotha's beds, believin that the essence of
what we need can be found between
someone else's legs and gettin some of whats between those legs is
paramount to our survival and we must survive. meanwhile, the more
guilty of us mouf off the most bout how it aint our fault if some women
dont know how to hold on to their men and anyway, if the situation was
reversed they'd be doing the same thing.

HE is not coming. and some of us are beginning to look hungrily at
each otha. and from past experiences with men, we kno what it is that
most of us need, and we try, in vain, to offer it to each otha. since there
arent enuff men to go around anyway, some of us try to make up for the
shortage by being synthetic men; while in children's eyes confusion can
be seen consuming the brain. and all that is truly redwhiteandblue
encourages us to continue this trend so that the race may hurry to its
end.

HE is not coming. so anything goes. anything
meaning white men who, just yesterday, cld storm into our quarters
kick our men out the bed and proceed to rape us. and now we send them
invitations to do the same thing. diahnn caroll has jumped from the t. v.
screen into our psyche to let us kno that white is where its at. and after
umpteen disillusionments with the bros who dont look like they came
outa GQ, who dont drive cute little foreign cars, or take us on trips to
the islands, we take the bait, accept a date, and hope that our newly
formed relationships will save the day they were
designed to destroy.

HE is not coming. and the overwhelming possibility of never havin
a family drives some sistahs into secretly planned one-sided pregnancies

that result in the
creation of one-sided children with reluctant fathers
who have no court in which to plea their cases but, who can be taken to
court for non-support of the childen they didnt mean to create. but then,
if they didnt mean to make them, why werent they doing something to
prevent them? but thats anotha riff reserved for anotha time. what we
wanna establish here is the possibility that:

HE is not coming. but some of us figure, he's just late. so we take
pills and smoke herb to help us wait. meanwhile, there are always
younger men to bless and caress at best. and it helps if u're a dancer, cuz
then u can skank some of the pain away while every day we all watch
amerika kill Black men.

HE is not coming, and those of us who kno this are
sometimes so shattered by so severe a reality, that we toss our minds into
the junk-heap of life, and end up walkin down terminal streets wearing
4 and 5 coats, sleeping on stairwells, and talkin to creatures only
visible under oppression. suicide statistics reach the top by climbing up
our backs as we eat ourselves to death, drug ourselves to death, and
stress ourselves right out over wants that will never be fulfilled.

HE is not coming. and if the HE u are waiting for, in
any way resembles prince, billy dee, jesse jackson or even smokey, then
u can forget it, cuz they are not ordinary men. they were chosen by
white people, for u to moon over, and spoon over, until u completely
missed the bros who were really available to u. at some time or anotha,
most of us have believed that a good man is hard to find. well, depends
on what u call good. and seldom have we looked for good in unstylish,
unattractive, unmacho men. yeah, we like our good to come all
wrapped up in sex, and money which is why so many of us are alone,
right now.

58

HE is not coming. and some of us take it personally.
we think somehow, that we have failed to be woman enuff. that maybe,
we shld say yes more, and no less. just to please and appease. maybe we
shld blink our eyes more, and read less to keep from showing signs of
intelligence, maybe we shld spreak eagle whenever they say and to hell
with how we really feel. and maybe we shld feel less, and act more. and
maybe we shld pay their bills, and cook their meals whenever they
hunger, and maybe we shldnt mind if they have 2 or 3 women on the
side. anything to please them. so they'll stay, and continue to be as
useless to and unappreciative of us as possible.

HE is not coming. but a workable situation can still be found if
sistahs wld stop actin like individuals and realize that their
man-problems are a collective problem shared by all otha sistahs. and
not unique, as some wld like to think. not just for the homely or the
lack-lustre, or the super-ordinary. and instead of sharpening our claws,
we shld be sharpening our minds. until we all realize that the imbalances
we are experiencing are as deliberate as klansmen in the whitehouse. the
bros we now choose from are the ones who escaped and survived the
many deaths planned for them: like nam, prison, mental
institutions, fratricide, and suicide. and since we kno these mines were
planted along our path to deter us from liberation,
our reaction must be to adapt; and sharing seems to be the only way

but not sharing as in sneaking.
not sharing as in lying.
not sharing as a result of some selfish penile
ultimatum.
not sharing as in diseases.
not sharing as in a gathering of vaginas.
not sharing as in assembly-line baby-making.
not sharing as in pimping.

59

*the only way there can be quality in our sharing is if we decide as women
that we luv each otha so much that we want all of us to have the right to
be part of a family. we have to decide that the race comes above all and
that the race is made up of families and that family can mean anything
we want it to. and if we continue to let white standards be the order of
the day, genocide will continue to be the order of the century.*

*HE is not coming. so lets luv the ones who come.
and whatever the race needs, lets do it.
whatever is best for the family, lets do it.
whatever ensures the greatest happiness for the greatest
number of people, lets do it.
and if all these things call for the sharing of our men
then — lets deal with it.*

White Traditions In Black-Face

Dark-skinned white people be rockin steady to a defunct and deactivating beat. week-end wonderlands find them sprawled across the amerikan landscape, speaking horatio algerically about the new and improved roles for Black idiots within the hierarchy of white nationalism. true-er than dobermans to their masters, they continuously compensate for their accidental births, by hating color of any kind. more accurate than dobermans they go for the jugular of the race by campaigning kama-kazi like against Black concerns.

and in the mendacious tradition of true whiteness
the halls of education are decorated like pigeon shit on windowsills, with Black skulls, while scattered about in strategic locations, the dark-skinned cross-overs sit like pompous mule hindparts,
administering miseducation and casually perpetuating death to Black intellect and afrikan life-forms. the green linings of their pockets paralyze and obliterate their senses; commitment to Black struggle is an aberration. the academic letters strungout behind their names spell out their betrayals in gothic terms of I-ness, Me-ness and Mine-ness. and they are so high on crossing over, they are beyond approach and reproach. they are in flight, above the quest to be free of niggerness. they are out there... flying so high, in such startling numbers, that soon, one day soon, we gonna havta declare open season on all Black buzzards.

and in the parasitic tradition of the ice-folks
Black carpetbaggers come fallin outa the sky like locusts, every four years. invisible, except during campaign seasons, the only thing we kno of them is the busy-signal they give when we try to ask for something more than free chicken on election nite.

and those who care, those who extend themselves to us, those who try to serve our battered interests, are veto'd into powerlessness by the cross-overs, who run and fetch better than lassie for a proverbial pat

from their pale pacificers. calling themselves the Black elite, the cross-
overs are guaranteed to support white policies no matter how they
strangle Black life. at a whistle, they will sit up, beg, bark, roll over, and
or bend over just to get a piece of the amerikan pie, which when fully
digested, maggotizes one's existence.

and in the exploitative tradition of zenocentric whiteness,
Minstrels in Blackface are pimped into international prominence, by
record companies that dont give a damn about a Black anything, so long
as it sings, dances and processes its hair. and even after filling these
requirements, some cross-overs feel it a matter of must, to have
corrective surgery done on their too Afrikan looking faces. and the noses
go from feast to famine, the hair goes from tiny clenched fists to dripping
clots of grease and the butterfly lips are reduced to beaks. such is the
star-studded road to success, the one the cross-overs keep trying to ease
on down. they travel in packs like wolves, spreading individualism like
herpes. forsaking all opportunities to uplift Black consciousness.
denying all responsibility to inspire Black liberation. and on the cash end
of our destruction, they dance and cohabitate with the enemy, while
spending our money on everything but us. and they try to tell us that
integration works, that it is possible to co-exist with whitey. only they
never say on which planet, cuz they sure aint talkin bout this one.

and in the christian tradition of heathenistic whiteness
Jesus, the naacp and blind Black devotion to the ministry, we who still
hold on to our eyes, see masses of impoverished people of color being
hustled year in, year out, by gigantic cross-overs with molasses running
outa the corners of their mouths. they wear religious objects around
their necks as if propinquity wld make their utterings seem more divinely
inspired. they are always claiming they represent us, but they dont live
with us. they always claimin to be one of us, but there aint a blade of
grass in all their roots. irridescent coons for white politicians, they try to
glitter us into the democratic party by assuring us that the donkey people
treat their nigras better than the elephant people do. and it never matters

that the two-party system is really one. it matters not, that Black people lose in every election no matter how many dark faces they manage to push into white spaces. nobody cares about us, and u can take that to the bank. no one, who is not one of us, will ever move significantly in the direction of our best Black interests. and by the way, have u cleaned out yr pulpit today? i say, watch who u kneel with, and keep a trigger eye on anybody who wants u to pray to any GOD that aint Black and electric like you.

and in the barren tradition of x-rated whiteness Superlies are magnified on the silver screen. false images jump bad on the t. v., will jump into yr livingroom and dare u to be yr Black self. cuz according to the tube, Black men are something to laugh at, Black children are something white people must adopt becuz Blacks dont want them, and Black women just wanna break, so they can forsake their own, and return to mammyhood with nell. here we are under invasion and we've got our other girlfriend runnin down to forsythe county to ask the invaders why they dont like us. we are in a state of war and cant even remember when the first shot was fired. everyday the enemy puts his faser on prime-time stun and we are bombarded with destructive, displays of divine trash. v. d. video-dementia, is in epidemic proportions among the young. symptoms of the disease can be seen in low-school attendance, poor study habits, drug abuse, too, too, too-soon premarital sex, teenage pregnancies, teenage killa-cide, teenage suicide, and other media-induced insanities.
for like the sexual disease, v. d. also leads to brain damage, by pumping bad values, and low morals into our homes, v. d. slowly eats away at the family structure by making singleness more desirable than a steady relationship; by making men look and act more like women and vice-a-versa; by featuring sex as a nightly goal rather than a spiritual connection; by combining sex with violence, instead of couplin sex with love. with the exception of a few videos, most come from the devil's workshop. they are more influential than the school system, more

63

church, more threating than goree island, and in the end, more deadly than aids. observe, if u will, the burnt-out youth, aspiring to be no more than a dmc look-alike. talk about desolation. but, are we talkin about desolation or tradition? that great white tradition of negating Black existence...

for it is only in the tradition of whiteness that we pour ourselves into skin-tight jeans, or fleshout in mini-skirts. only in their tradition do we dye our hair blond, maroon, flaming orange, or punk blue like betty-boo. some of us even draw arrows into our hair to point to where our brains ustah be.

it is only in the tradition of whiteness that we straighten, maim and kill our hair. only in their tradition, that we make up our already made-up faces, purple-ize our brown eyes, redden our already colorful cheeks and goo-down our already accented lips.

IN THE HEART OF THE BUSH, THESE THINGS ARE UNTHOUGHT OF... IN THE SACRED BASTIONS OF BLACK AESTHETICS, THESE PHENOMENA RING A DEATH KNELL THROUGHOUT THE SOUL.

for it is only in the tradition of whiteness that we marry our slavemasters, or mate with our oppressors. only in their tradition do we lower ourselves to be equal to them by marrying one of their kind. only in their tradition can we achieve national scumdom by allowing ourselves to represent amerika and allowing photos to be taken of white tongues pointing cobra-like at our black crotches and legendary behinds. white tradition forces us to live un-natural lives and die humiliating deaths while being captive to the steady rhythm of a petrified beat. we are marching into oblivion, a total white-out. the end of funky elegance. the jack-the-ripper death of soul.

in Afrika, death is represented by whiteness. pity, we didnt kno that meant people too. it was being ripped apart from the Afrikan tradition that made us go mad, made us think we were our own enemies, made us claw at our own flesh. and being slashed away from the Afrikan tradition, left us with huge gashes in our spiritual sides, we roam the earth like wounded animals, barely conscious of our own actions. almost dead to the fact that the Afrikan tradition still exists and it is only within the definition of Afrikan tradition that we can find identity, purpose and direction. only the Afrikan tradition can tell us how to lift the race; preserve it; rejuvenate it; reproduce it; and forever protect it against the onslaught of white traditions.

In the beginning, the world was sustained upon Afrikan tradition becuz there were no others. and out of that universal body of knowledge came all knowledge. music was born when the first black joints were clicked into place. Black folks and music have always existed simultaneously, needing each other for honing and ultimate perfection.

in the Afrikan tradition, we are constantly re-hued while constantly being bleached. in the Afrikan tradition, we are always moving towards the good, while being defined as the bad. in the Afrikan tradition, we survive the unsurvivable, reach over the insurmountable, break-thru the impenetrable, to do a victory tour that will last the length of time. but the Afrikan tradition cannot function by itself. cannot feed itself. must have the support of Black people everywhere to kick butt on its behalf. the Afrikan tradition needs believers to mojo us into immortality. the Afrikan tradition needs fighters to free us from the flashy death of white traditions. the Afrikan tradition
needs YOU.